TREY and NASH
To
GreatGrandmother McPherson (Mac)
From
7-20-2014
Date

Standard
BIBLE STORYBOOK SERIES

EGYPT
TO THE PROMISED LAND

Retold by Carolyn Larsen

Standard®
PUBLISHING

Cincinnati, Ohio

Published by Standard Publishing, Cincinnati, Ohio
www.standardpub.com
Copyright © 2012 by Standard Publishing

Printed in: China

Project editors: Elaina Meyers, Dawn A. Medill, and Marcy Levering
Cover design: Dale Meyers

Illustrations from Standard Publishing's Classic Bible Art Collection

ISBN 978-0-7847-3564-0

Library of Congress Cataloging-in-Publication Data

Larsen, Carolyn, 1950-
  Egypt to the promised land / retold by Carolyn Larsen.
    p. cm.
  ISBN 978-0-7847-3564-0 (hardcover)
1. Exodus, The--Juvenile literature. 2. Bible stories, English--O.T.
Exodus. 3. Bible stories, English--O.T. Pentateuch. 4. Bible stories,
English--O.T. Joshua. I. Title.
  BS680.E9L37 2012
  222'.1209505--dc23
                              2012002483

17 16 15 14 13 12   1 2 3 4 5 6 7 8 9

LEAVING EGYPT

Hundreds of years after Joseph's family moved to Egypt, God sent a shepherd named Moses to lead His people out. God used Moses and some special signs to convince Pharaoh to let the people leave. The signs were very unpleasant, and only after the death of the firstborn male in every household—even Pharaoh's—was Pharaoh convinced to let the Israelites leave Egypt.

Crossing the Red Sea *Exodus 13:17—14:31*

Pharaoh let the Israelites leave Egypt after the tenth plague. In fact that last plague was so terrible that the Egyptians could not wait for them to leave. Moses led thousands of Israelites as they left Egypt and God's presence was with them the whole way. If anyone ever felt afraid that maybe God had left them, all they had to do was look ahead. In the daytime a tall column of cloud led them, and at night the column turned to a fire. The Israelites followed this column because they knew it was God's presence. They followed it day and night until God told them to stop and camp. Their camp was right on the shoreline of the Red Sea. That's when they discovered that Pharaoh had

changed his mind about letting them leave. He got into his chariot and commanded his soldiers and all the chariots in his army to catch the Israelites and bring them back to Egypt. He didn't want to lose all his slaves. As Pharaoh

and his army approached their camp, the Israelites started to panic. They backed up as far as they could, but they were on the shores of the sea. The army was behind them and the sea was in front of them. They were trapped!

The Israelites were terrified and they focused their fear at Moses. "Why did you take us out of Egypt?" they screamed at him. "We were safe there. We are just going to die out here in the wilderness. Slavery in Egypt was better than dying out here!"

Moses tried to calm the people down. "Don't be afraid," he said. "Just wait and see what God is going to do to protect you!" The angel of the Lord moved the column of cloud around behind the Israelites so the Egyptians couldn't see them. Then God told Moses to hold his shepherd's staff out over the Red Sea. When he did, a powerful wind came and moved the waters of the sea. The water swished and swirled as it divided into two large walls of water with dry ground between them. "Move," Moses told the Israelites, and they began to cross the Red Sea on dry land with walls of water on either side of them. It took all night to cross the sea. The column of cloud turned to fire to lead the people across but still the Egyptians couldn't see them.

When the Egyptian chariots and army entered on the other side, they thought they could rush in and capture the Israelites. God saw what they were trying to do so He made the wheels of their chariots fall off and He threw the soldiers into confusion so they were running into each other or running the wrong way. Then God told Moses to stretch out his hand over the sea again, and when he did the water of the Red Sea began to crash back together into its normal place. Every chariot was covered by water. The entire Egyptian army drowned that day in the Red Sea but every single Israelite safely reached the other side of the sea.

Food from Heaven *Exodus 16*

After God miraculously led the Israelites through the Red Sea and saved them from the Egyptians, they traveled in the wilderness. Day after day, week after week, they walked and walked. Before long the food they had brought along from Egypt was gone. The people were tired and hungry and even though God had done amazing miracles to free them

from slavery and save them from the Egyptian army, they started complaining and whining. "Moses, why did you even take us out of Egypt? At least we had food there. We're going to starve to death out here in the wilderness."

God heard the people's complaints and He spoke to Moses. "I'm going to send food down from Heaven for the people. They can go out each day and pick up all the food they need for that day. However, I'm going to give them

9

a test to see if they will follow my rules. Tell them to pick up only what they need for their families each day except on the sixth day when they should pick up twice what they need. No food will come on the seventh day."

Moses called all the people together and said, "Every night you will have proof that it was God himself who led you out of Egypt. Every morning you will see proof of His presence with you. He has heard your complaining, which is against Him, not against Aaron or me. God promises to give you meat to eat every evening and bread every morning. This is His promise to you."

That very evening hundreds and hundreds of quail flew into the camp and landed on the ground. The people could capture them without even trying very hard. The next morning when the people got up the ground was wet with dew. As the dew dried up, thin white flakes were left on the ground. The Israelites were confused. "What is this?" they asked.

Moses answered, "It is the bread God promised you. Here is His instruction: Pick up only what you need for your family for this day." It would be about two quarts for each person. By obeying God's instructions each person had just enough to eat. But Moses warned the people, "Do not try to pick up extra to keep overnight." Of course some people tried to do that, but by the next morning it was rotted, full of bugs, and very, very stinky.

Every day the people picked up what they needed and any flakes left on the ground melted away in the sun. On the sixth day there was extra manna (that's what the flakes were called) so the people picked up enough to last them for two days. That's what God told them to do because the seventh day was to be a day of rest. The manna was sweet and tasted like honey cakes. Between the quail and the manna, the people had plenty of food to eat. God sent manna six days a week for 40 years—until the people were settled in the land of Canaan where they could grow their own crops.

Water from a Rock *Exodus 17:1-7*

A little while after God began sending manna and quail to the people, He told them to break camp and start walking again. They still needed to get to the land God had promised to give them. The people traveled as far as a place called Rephidim but there was no water there. Right away the people started complaining to Moses, "Give us water

to drink! Why did you take us out of Egypt? We had plenty of water there. We're all going to die out here with no water to drink!" Moses tried to remind them of all the miracles God had already done to take care of them. But they just wanted to complain.

"Quiet!" Moses cried. "Why are you arguing with me? Why are you complaining against God?"

The people kept complaining so Moses turned to God and asked, "What do I do with these people? They are going to come after me with stones!"

God said, "Take your shepherd's staff, the same one that you used when you struck the waters of the Nile River and I turned them to blood. Call the leaders of the people to come with you and walk on ahead of the people. I will meet with you by a large rock near Mt. Sinai. Hit the rock with your staff and I will make water pour out of it. The people will be able to drink as much water as they want. Then they will stop complaining."

Moses did what God told him to do and the people had all the water they wanted. Moses named that place *Massah* which means "the place of testing" and *Meribah* which means "the place of arguing" because the people argued with Moses by asking whether or not God was going to take care of them.

The Ten Commandments *Exodus 20*

It had been two months since the Israelites left Egypt. After they left Rephidim, the place where water came from a rock, God called Moses to come up to the top of Mt. Sinai. He wanted to talk to Moses alone because He had special rules for the people about how they should live. God wanted Moses to take the rules to the people and get commitments from

them to live by these rules. The people were not allowed to go up the mountain with Moses or even get close to the mountain.

These rules that God gave Moses are called the Ten Commandments.

They are:
1. Do not worship any other gods besides God.
2. Do not make any idols to worship because God is a jealous God and won't share your worship.

14

3. Do not use the name of the Lord your God in a bad way. You will be punished if you do.
4. Keep the Sabbath day holy. You can work six days a week, but rest on the seventh day.
5. Honor your father and your mother, then you will live a long life.
6. Do not murder.
7. Do not commit adultery.
8. Do not steal.
9. Do not lie about your neighbor.
10. Do not want what your neighbor has.

God delivered these rules to Moses with a crash of thunder and the loud blast of a horn. Smoke and lightning billowed from the mountain and the people were very afraid. God wrote them on stone tablets with His own hand. Moses took the tablets down to the people and told them what they said and the people agreed to live by these rules.

The Golden Calf *Exodus 32*

God called Moses to come up on Mt. Sinai for a private meeting, so Moses left Aaron in charge of the people. Moses was gone for a long time. In fact he was gone so long that the people didn't think he was going to come back at all. So they went to Aaron and said, "We need a god who can lead us. Moses has disappeared and we don't think he is even coming back. Make a god for us!"

Aaron said, "OK, everyone take off any gold jewelry you are wearing and bring it to me." All the people obeyed Aaron, and he soon had a large pile of gold jewelry in front of him. Aaron put the gold in a pot and melted it down to liquid. Then he molded and formed

the liquid gold into the shape of a calf. When the people saw it they cheered and cried, "This is the god who brought us out of Egypt." Aaron saw how excited the people were about the golden calf. He built an altar and announced that the next day there would be a festival in honor of the Lord.

The people were very excited and they got up early to sacrifice burnt offerings and peace offerings. They celebrated with feasts and drinking and many kinds of behaviors that did not please God.

Meanwhile, up on Mt. Sinai, God knew what was going on with the people. "Moses, go back down the mountain to your people. They have done something terrible. They agreed to live by my Ten Commandments but they are already disobeying me. They have made an idol that looks like a golden calf and are worshipping it and making sacrifices to it. They are saying that this god is who brought them out of Egypt. Moses, leave me alone now so that my anger can rage against these people. I will destroy all of them and I will make you, Moses, into a great nation!"

Moses couldn't believe what the people had done. He was angry and disappointed too, but he begged God to spare the people. "O God," he said, "You brought these people out of slavery in Egypt. You have done miracles to save them and You said that You would make their descendants as many as there are stars in the sky. O God, You promised to give the land of Canaan to these people. Please God, remember Your covenant with these people."

So God took back His threat to destroy the people. Moses went down the mountain, carrying the two stone tablets with the rules for how the people should live. When he got to the camp, he saw the calf and saw the people dancing. He threw the tablets to the ground in anger and they broke into pieces.

Moses took the golden calf, melted it in a fire, and then ground the gold into powder. He mixed the powder with water and made the people drink it. Then he turned to Aaron and asked, "What were you thinking? Why did you do this?"

"Don't get so upset. I just threw their gold jewelry into the fire and this calf is what came out," Aaron lied.

Moses saw that the people were disobedient so he said, "Any of you who are on the Lord's side with me, come stand over here!" The whole tribe of Levi came and from that day on they were the tribe who served God.

The Twelve Spies *Numbers 13, 14*

The Israelites had walked and walked as God led them through the wilderness to the land of Canaan. It was the land He promised to give to them when He had Moses lead them out of Egypt. As the whole nation of Israel camped at the edge of the land of Canaan, God told Moses to send one leader from each tribe into Canaan to explore it and report back. So Moses sent twelve men into Canaan to explore the land. He especially wanted to know about the people who lived there. He wanted to know if they were tall or if they looked very strong. It was important to know

18

if there were many people in the land or only a few. The spies should find out if the soil was healthy and grew good crops and they should also see what kinds of crops and fruits grew there. Moses told them to find out everything they could about the land of Canaan. So the spies sneaked into the land and then explored it. They came to one place where grapes grew and the spies cut down a huge cluster of big, juicy grapes to take back and show Moses. They took samples of other kinds of fruits they found too.

The spies searched out the land for 40 days and then returned to Moses to give their reports. The entire nation of Israel gathered to hear what the spies had to say about the land of Canaan. The spies showed the fruit they had gathered. They told Moses and the people, "The land of Canaan is magnificent. The soil is healthy and it grows big and healthy crops like we've never seen before. But the people living there are like giants."

Ten of the spies said, "We felt like grasshoppers next to the people of Canaan. They are strong and powerful. The cities have strong walls around them. There is no way that we could take this land because the cities are protected and the people are more powerful than we are."

But two spies, Joshua and Caleb, said, "Yes, the people of Canaan are big and strong. Yes, there are many of them, but we can win against them. After all, we have God on our side. Come on, people, and be courageous. We can do it!" However, even though the people had seen God do many amazing miracles for them, they listened to the 10 frightened spies instead of the two courageous spies. They refused to try to take the land of Canaan.

Because God was not pleased that the Israelites did not trust Him, He said that the present generation of Israelites would die before the nation was ever allowed to enter the promised land. The whole nation would wander in the wilderness for 40 years. Only Joshua and Caleb, the two hopeful spies, would be allowed to enter the promised land.

The Bronze Serpent *Numbers 21:4-9*

As the people of Israel wandered through the wilderness—because of their punishment for not trusting God and taking the land when God first led them there—they were once more near the Red Sea. The people got impatient with the round-about route they were taking. They were tired of walking and just wanted to be in the new land. They started complaining against Moses and Aaron once again. "Why have you led us out here to the wilderness to die?" they cried. "Why didn't you just leave us alone in Egypt?" Never mind that they were slaves in Egypt! "There is nothing to eat here. We don't have anything to drink either! We are sick to death of this manna too!"

God was tired of the complaining. He was sad that the people kept forgetting all the miracles He had done for them. So He sent poisonous snakes slithering among the people. Many people were bitten and some of them died. The people immediately came to Moses and cried, "We've sinned! We're sorry that we spoke against God and against you. Please, pray that God will forgive us. Ask Him to take away the snakes!" Moses listened and prayed for the people.

So God told Moses to make a snake out of bronze. It should look just like the snakes that were biting and killing the people. "Attach the bronze snake to a pole and post it among the people. Anyone who is bitten by the snakes but looks at the bronze snake you have made will live."

Moses did what God told him to do. The people who looked at the bronze snake, as God instructed, were healed from the snakebites.

THE STORY OF JOSHUA

Moses led God's people out of Egypt just as God asked him to do. It wasn't easy because every time something went wrong or took longer than they thought it should, the people turned on Moses and complained and whined. One time Moses' patience with the people was completely gone and when God told him what to do, Moses disobeyed. Because of his disobedience, Moses was not allowed to enter the promised land. For 40 years Moses led the people to the promised land, but he never got to step inside it. God did, however, let Moses see the land. A new leader was chosen to lead the Israelites into the promised land. His name was Joshua.

A New Leader *Deuteronomy 31:1-8; 34:1-9*

When Moses was 120 years old, God told him it was time for him to step aside as the leader of the Israelites. God also told Moses, "I will cross over the Jordan ahead of the people. I will destroy the people and nations living there and help your people take possession of the land."

The Israelites waited expectantly to hear if God would appoint a new leader or if they would choose their own. God had already made that decision. Joshua would be the new leader of the Israelite nation. Moses announced that Joshua was his replacement. He said that God promised them that Joshua would lead them. "Be brave and strong," Moses commanded

the people, "because God is with you. He will never fail you!"

Moses called Joshua to come up in front of all the people. "Joshua, God has chosen you to be the new leader of these people. Be strong and courageous because you will lead these people into the land God promised to give their ancestors. You are the one who will lead them into the fulfillment of that promise. God is with you. He will always be with you."

Soon after that, Moses went to Mount Nebo and climbed up to the top. God let Moses see the whole promised land. "This is the land I promised to Abraham, Isaac, and Jacob," God said. "I promised I would

give it to their descendants. I'm allowing you to see it, but you cannot enter it." Moses died up on that mountain and no one knows where God buried his body.

Joshua took over leadership of the Israelites. The people listened to him and obeyed him. They knew that God had appointed him and that God would be with Joshua as he led them. God had one strong commandment for Joshua, "Obey all the laws that Moses gave you. Study the Book of the Law continually. Think about it day and night so that you will know when you are obeying or disobeying it. Only by obeying it will you succeed."

A Woman Named Rahab *Joshua 2*

G od's first job for Joshua was to actually bring the people into the promised land. They had been moving toward that for 40 long years. The city of Jericho was the first place God wanted them to capture so Joshua sent two spies into that city to check things out. The spies crept into the city, thinking no one noticed them, and they went to the home of a woman named Rahab, who did not serve God. Some people saw the two spies sneak into Jericho and those people hurried to tell the king about them. The king immediately sent a message to Rahab, "Bring out those two men who are hiding in your house because they are spies sent here by our enemies to check out our city."

But Rahab had already thought that the king might ask this so she had hidden the spies on her rooftop. She sent this message back to him: "Yes, those two men were here but I didn't realize they were spies. As the city gate was being closed at sunset, they left the city. I don't know where they went, but if you send your soldiers out quickly, you may find them." Actually, Rahab had hidden the spies beneath some stalks of flax that were on her rooftop.

Even if the king's men had gone up to the roof, they would not have seen the spies. Instead, though, the king's men rushed through the city gates and went to search for the two spies.

After the king's men left, Rahab went back up to the roof to talk with the spies. "I know your God has given you this land. I know you will capture this city. The people of Jericho are terrified of you. We've heard how your God parted the Red Sea to get your people through it and then crashed the waters down on the Egyptian army. All of our hearts shook with fear when we heard that and other stories of how He protected you. I'm asking you to show kindness and protection to me and my family since I have protected you. When you capture this city will you spare our lives? Give me a sign so that I know I can trust you."

"We will honor your kindness to us," the spies promised. "We will make sure you and your family are spared."

Rahab used a rope to let the men down over the city wall through her window. "Run into the nearby hills and hide for three days," she told them. By then the king's men would stop searching for them and it would be safe for

them to go back to Joshua and the rest of the Israelites.

Before they left, the spies said to Rahab, "Hang a red cord in your window so that we will know which house is yours when we come to take Jericho. If you don't do that, our promise to spare you and your family does not stand. If any of your family leaves the house and goes out into the street when we are taking the city, we cannot promise their safety."

Rahab agreed and hung the red cord in her window right away. The spies hid in the hills for three days then returned to Joshua to report on the city. They said, "We can take the city of Jericho. God has promised it to us and the people there are afraid of us because of Him."

The Fall of Jericho *Joshua 3, 4, 6*

T he first step to capturing Jericho was to cross over the Jordan River. However, it was at flood stage, so how would the people get across? God told Joshua exactly what to do. He had the priests carry the ark of the covenant into the edge of the river's waters. The people watched and waited as they did that. When their feet touched the water, the

river water backed up into a pile and made a dry space for the Israelites to cross. The priests stood there until every Israelite had crossed the riverbed. Then they brought the ark of the covenant out of the river and the waters crashed back into place at flood stage as before. Joshua had leaders from the 12 tribes set up stones on the shore of the river as an altar of praise for God protecting them.

When the Israelites reached Jericho, it was shut up tight. The gates were locked and there was no sign of life inside the walls. God assured Joshua that the city would fall to his army. He gave Joshua specific instructions on how to approach the battle. "March all the way around the city walls once a day with all your soldiers. Do this for six days," God said. "This is the order you should march in: The armed soldiers will lead the group and then seven priests each carrying a trumpet are next. Behind them is the ark of the covenant and another guard unit is behind it. The priests should blow their horns as you march, but the people must be completely quiet."

Joshua explained the plan to the people and emphasized, "You've got to be completely quiet until I give you the sign, then you shout for all you're worth!" They marched once a day for six days. The people inside Jericho must have wondered what they were up to. On the seventh day Joshua's people marched around the city seven times, just as God instructed. But on the seventh time around, Joshua gave a sign and all the people shouted! When they did, the great walls of Jericho crumbled and fell down. Joshua's soldiers climbed over the fallen walls and ran in to capture the city. The two spies remembered to look for the red cord in Rahab's window. They found it and led her and her family to safety just as they promised they would. Rahab stayed with the Israelites for the rest of her life.

From that time on, none of the people questioned Joshua's leadership of their nation.

The Sun Stands Still *Joshua 10:1-15*

J oshua and the Israelites set up camp near the people of Gibeon. Joshua and the king of Gibeon made an agreement that their people would live in peace with one another. That was fine until the king of Jerusalem realized that the Gibeonites and Israelites were friends. He was worried that the two nations might get together and declare war on

his people. So the king of Jerusalem got four other kings of nearby nations to join him in declaring war on Gibeon. They thought they would beat the Gibeonites at their own plan.

As soon as the five nations Attacked, the men of Gibeon sent an urgent message to Joshua. "Help us!" they cried. "Don't desert us now when these five armies are attacking us. Help!" Joshua didn't ignore them. He marched his army right up to where the battle was raging.

God told Joshua, "Don't be afraid of them. I am delivering these five nations into your hands. You will win and not one of them will be left standing!"

It took all night for Joshua's army to reach the battlefield but when they did they took their enemies by surprise. The Lord caused the enemy soldiers to become confused and Joshua's army easily defeated them. His army chased the soldiers away, and as they were running, God sent a hailstorm on them. The large hailstones killed more of the enemy soldiers than Joshua's soldiers did.

During the battle, Joshua stood before all the Israelites and said to God, "Make the sun stand still. Hold back the moon so that we can have complete victory today!" So God made the sun stop in the middle of the sky and stand still for a full day! There has never been another day like that. Everyone knew that God was fighting for Israel.